Pebble® MATH

It's a Shape!

by M. W. Penn

Consulting Editor: Gail Saunders-Smith, PhD

CAPSTONE PRESS
a capstone imprint

Pebble Books are published by Capstone Press,
151 Good Counsel Drive, P.O. Box 669, Mankato, Minnesota 56002.
www.capstonepub.com

Books published by Capstone Press are manufactured with paper
containing at least 10 percent post-consumer waste.

Library of Congress Cataloging-in-Publication Data
Penn, M. W. (Marianne W.), 1944–
  It's a shape! / by M.W. Penn.
    p. cm. — (Pebble books. Pebble math)
  Summary: "Simple rhyming text and color photographs describe shapes"—
Provided by publisher.
  Includes bibliographical references and index.
  ISBN 978-1-4296-6040-2 (library binding)
  ISBN 978-1-4296-7068-5 (paperback)
  1. Shapes—Juvenile literature. I. Title. II. Series.
  QA445.5.P455 2012
  516'.15—dc22   2011003297

Note to Parents and Teachers

The Pebble Math set supports national mathematics standards
related to algebra and geometry. This book describes and illustrates
shapes. The images support early readers in understanding the
text. The repetition of words and phrases helps early readers
learn new words. This book also introduces early readers to
subject-specific vocabulary words, which are defined in the
Glossary section. Early readers may need assistance to read some
words and to use the Table of Contents, Glossary, Read More,
Internet Sites, and Index sections of the book.

Printed in the United States of America in North Mankato, Minnesota.
032011   006110CGF11

Table of Contents

4

What Are Shapes?

Shapes on the bed,

Shapes on the wall.

Straight shapes and curvy shapes,

Big shapes and small.

6

Shapes are wide or narrow,

Shapes are short or tall.

But shapes are just flat

With no thickness at all!

NO PASSING ZONE

STOP

DEAD END

8

Polygons

All polygons have corners
And sides that are straight.
They have 3 sides or 4 sides
Or more sides—like 8!

What is a triangle?

Here is a clue:

It has 3 straight sides

And 3 corners too.

If a shape has 4 corners

Just exactly the same

And has 4 straight sides,

Rectangle is its name.

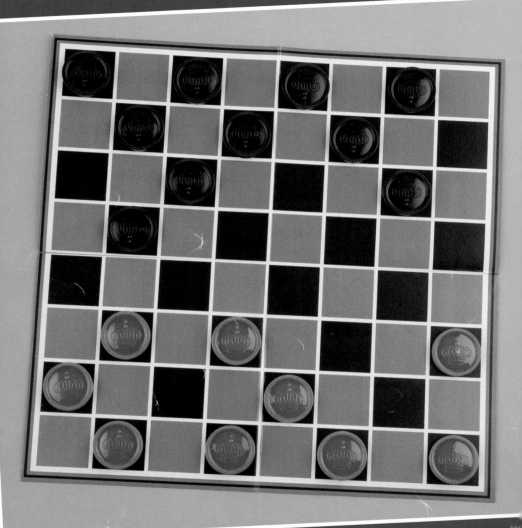

A special rectangle
With 4 equal sides,
A square is a shape
Just as tall as it's wide.

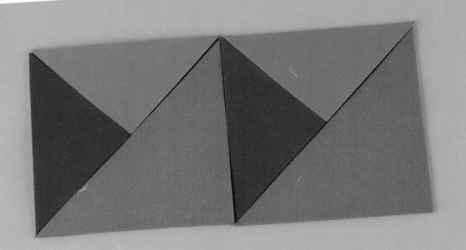

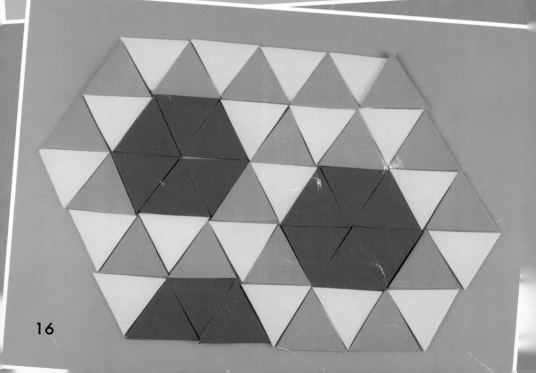

When you fit them together
Or pull them apart,
You can make polygons
Into colorful art.

Circles

A circle is just like

A tire or a hoop:

A perfectly round and

Unending loop.

Shapes All Around

Circle, triangle,

Rectangle, square—

Look at this picture

And find each one there.

Glossary

circle—a perfectly round loop

polygon—a flat shape whose sides are all straight lines

rectangle—a polygon with four sides and four equal corners

shape—a flat figure that is surrounded by straight lines, by curves, or by a combination of straight lines and curves

square—a rectangle with four sides exactly the same length

triangle—a flat shape with three straight sides and three corners

Read More

Aboff, Marcie. *If You Were a Polygon.* Math Fun. Minneapolis: Picture Window Books, 2010.

Dilkes, D. H. *I See Rectangles.* All about Shapes. Berkeley Heights, N.J.: Enslow Pub., 2011.

Steffora, Tracey. *Shapes in the Kitchen.* Math around Us. Chicago: Heinemann Library, 2011.

Internet Sites

FactHound offers a safe, fun way to find Internet sites related to this book. All of the sites on FactHound have been researched by our staff.

Here's all you do:

Visit *www.facthound.com*

Type in this code: 9781429660402

Index

Word Count: 157
Grade: 1
Early-Intervention Level: 11

Editorial Credits
Gillia Olson, editor; Juliette Peters, designer; Sarah Schuette, photo stylist;
   Marcy Morin, studio scheduler; Laura Manthe, production specialist

Photo Credits
Capstone Press/Juliette Peters, 6; Karon Dubke, cover and interior photographs
Image Farm, 8

The author would like to dedicate this book to Duncan Robinson, CBE, Master of
Magdalene College, Cambridge, UK.